Copyright © 2018 by MunaiiBookworks
All rights reserved. This book or any portion thereof
may not be reproduced or used in any manner whatsoever
without the express written permission of the publisher
except for the use of brief quotations in a book review.

Printed in the United States of America
First Printing, 2018
ISBN: 978-0-9861018-7-8

MunaiiBookworks
16192 Coastal Hwy, Lewes, DE 19958, USA
www.munaii.com

Writing Mastery
Personal Narrative

Contents

Introduction	2
Writing checklist	4
Complete the essay in your best writing	5
Writing Favorites	6
What is a personal narrative?	7
Writing prompts	8
The Writing Process	10
Quotes about Writing and life	12
Understanding the Question	13
Brainstorming	14
Generating Ideas	15
Place	16
Memory from a Thing	17
The Egg Story	18
Zooming in	21
Planning	23
Exciting Beginnings	24
Transition list	26
Transitions	27
First Draft	28
Proof Reading tags	30
Types of sentences	31
Mastering Figurative Language	32
The Power of Details	34
Mastering Show Don't Tell	36
Conclusions	38
Final draft	39
Sample Essay	41
Resources	42
Congratulations!	43

Introduction

The narrative writing program is the first of four writing courses in the Authorkid program. Everything you learn will help you in all aspects of your writing endeavours. Follow along each lesson and pause to complete the activities that can be found in your Writing Mastery Journal. You may also use your own composition book or computer to write your essays.

In order to successfully earn your certificate for the course, your final draft and five projects and all activities are to be completed.

WRITING CHECKLIST

CHECKING MY WRITING	1	2	3	4	5
Exciting Lead					
Egg Story					
5 Or more paragraphs- Did I indent?					
Quotations					
Spellings					
Details using sight					
Details using hearing/smell/touch					
Details using thinking					
Actions					
Feelings					
Proper Sequence					
Quotation marks- Start a new line with each speaker?					
Grammar and punctuation					
Does it make sense?					
Does it have a good ending?					
Is it interesting?					
Transitions and sentence variety					
Show don't tell					
Similes and Metaphors					
Sentence and word variety					
Total					

WRITING MASTERY

COMPLETE THE ESSAY IN YOUR BEST WRITING

MANY events have defined who I am. Write a brief essay to describe an event that tells us the kind of person you are.

Title _____

_____
_____
_____
_____
_____
_____
_____
_____
_____
_____
_____
_____
_____
_____
_____
_____
_____
_____
_____

WRITING FAVORITES

What do you like to write? Describe your best writing moments in each of the hearts.

WRITING MASTERY

What is a Personal Narrative?

Write your answer in the space below. Be sure to revise your thoughts after finishing this course.

_____

_____

_____

_____

_____

_____

_____

_____

_____

_____

WRITING MASTERY

WRITING PROMPTS

Tell a Story About…
1. Your first day of school.
2. Your most exciting day of school
3. A field trip that your class took.
4. Your favorite summer vacation.
5. A trip that included something unexpected or surprising.
6. A time that you experienced something spooky.
7. A time that you experienced something truly frightening.
8. A time that you learned something new that changed you in some way.
9. The moment when you met someone who changed your life.
10. The day that you got your first pet.
11. A move from one place to another.
12. Something funny that happened to you.
13. Something funny that happened to one of your family members or friends.
14. Something embarrassing that happened to you.
15. Your favorite birthday party.
16. A birthday that was disappointing.
17. A big storm (rain, snow or even a tornado!).
18. A time that the power went out.
19. A summer day when the temperature got much higher than expected.
20. A time when you went to an amusement park.
21. A time when you got lost somewhere.
22. A memorable experience with a favorite family member.
23. A sad experience with someone about whom you care.
24. Your most exciting moment playing sports.
25. Your most exciting moment performing in a play, singing, playing music or dancing.
26. An experience that left you feeling frustrated.
27. An experience that was hard but ended up being worth it.
28. A time that you experienced rejection.
29. A weird encounter with a stranger.
30. A random act of kindness.
31. A time that you took a stand for someone or for an issue that you care about.
32. A moment when you thought you might get hurt but didn't.
33. Breaking a bone (or otherwise suffering an injury).
34. Your first time away from home for the night (or longer).
35. A time when you experienced a historic event.
35. A time when you experienced a historic event.
36. Where you were when a major event happened. (Note: You don't need to have been at the site of the event; this prompt is about where you were when you found out about the event and how you reacted.)
37. A time when you rebelled against your parents or teacher.
38. A dangerous experience.

WRITING MASTERY | 8

39. A misunderstanding between yourself and someone else.
40. A difficult decision that you had to make.
41. The end of a friendship or relationship.
42. The beginning of a friendship or relationship.
43. A time when you judged someone first and then realized that you were wrong about the person.
44. A time when someone judged you first and then realized that he or she was wrong about you.
45. A moment when you felt that you were starting to grow up.
46. A time when you saw one or both of your parents in a different light.
47. A time when you looked up to your older sibling.
48. A time when your younger sibling looked up to you.
49. A time when you were grateful to be an only child.
50. An experience that you think has only ever happened to you!

Think about how people often feel excited or nervous when they do something new.

Write a personal narrative about a memorable first experience. . .

BE SURE TO

- Describe events of the experience with a clear focus
- provide a clear, beginning, middle, and end.
- Describe how this experience affected you.

ALWAYS PUT YOUR BEST EFFORT.

WRITING MASTERY

THE WRITING PROCESS

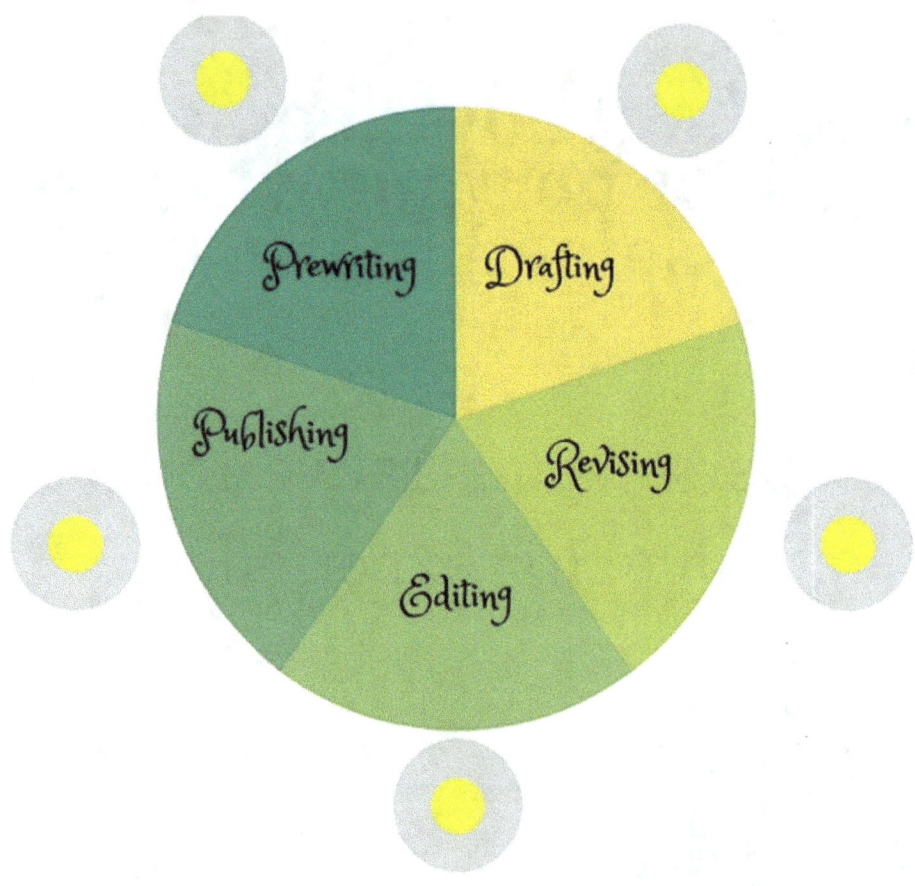

What happens at each stage of the writing process? State why it's important.

_____
_____
_____
_____
_____
_____

PROJECT 1

Poster
Create a poster or mobile or any other Interesting artifact to show your understanding of the writing process. Post a video explaining your work.

QUOTES ABOUT WRITING AND LIFE

Pick one quote that applies to your life or one event in your life. Write a personal story about it.

1. "We know what we are but know not what we may be." – Shakespeare
2. "Wheresoever you go, go with all your heart." – Confucius
3. "Don't cry because it's over, smile because it happened." – Dr. Seuss
4. "Yesterday is history. Tomorrow is a mystery. Today is a gift. That's why we call it 'The Present'." – Eleanor Roosevelt
5. "Fall seven times, stand up eight." – Japanese Proverb
6. "What one can be one must be." – Unknown
7. "Life is a gift."
8. "Not only must we be good, but we must also be good for something." – Henry David Thoreau
9. "You've got to do your own growing, no matter how tall your grandfather was." – Irish Proverb
10. "We make a living by what we get, but we make a life by what we give." – Winston Churchill
11. "Row, row, row your boat. Gently down the stream. Merrily, merrily, merrily, merrily, life is but a dream." – Alice Munro
12. "I am only one, but I am one. I cannot do everything, but I can do something. And I will not let what I cannot do interfere with what I can do." – Edward Everett Hale

Ray Bradbury

Just write every day of your life. Read intensely then see what happens.

Anne Frank

I can shake off everything as I write. My sorrows disappear. My courage is reborn."

Maya Angelou

There is no greater agony than bearing an untold story inside of you.

WRITING MASTERY

 # UNDERSTANDING THE QUESTION

If you are given a prompt, you want to read it and then write it out again in your own words. It's important that you understand the question being asked before you start answering.

Pick 5 questions on the writing prompts page and rewrite them in your own words. You may begin by saying, "I am going to write about…."

PERSONAL NARRATIVE
1
2
3
4
5

WRITING MASTERY | 13

BRAINSTORMING

Use the graphic organizer to brainstorm any ONE of the following topics
Favorite movies, Best places, Wild animals, Gadgets I love,

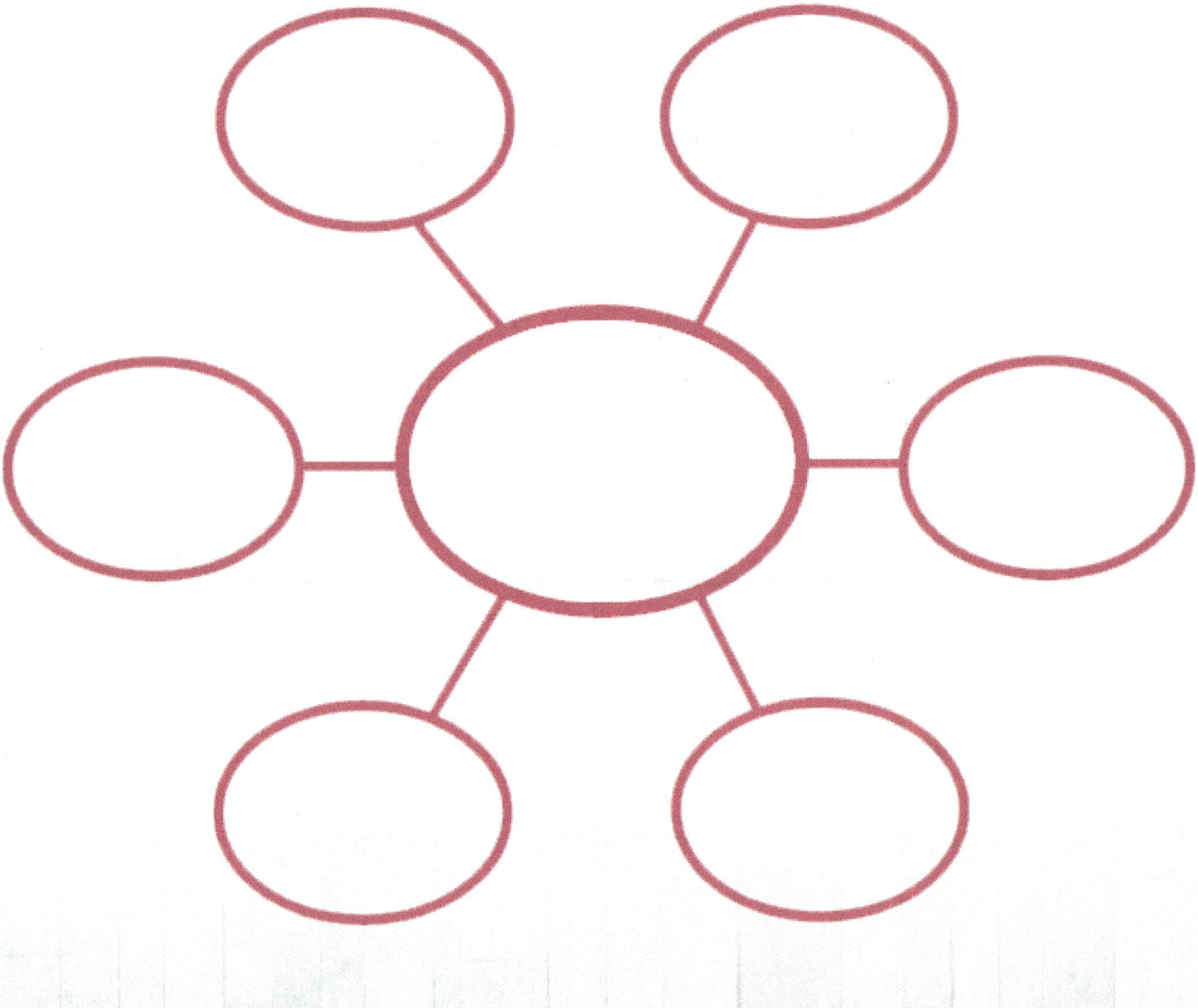

WRITING MASTERY

Generating Ideas
PERSON

Sometimes when you get an essay topic it's very difficult to come up with ideas. I suggest you think of all the people that you know. Write down a list of people on one side and then from that list, pick one person and then write down all the moments you have with them. This is one way to generate ideas.

People I Know

PLACE

Brain storm all the places that mean something to you.

Now pick one place and think of a special moment from that place.
Write memory in detail by zooming in.

MEMORY FROM A THING

Things in my life

4 special memories from one thing

WRITING MASTERY

THE EGG STORY

Can you eat a dozen eggs at once?
No! I didn't think so.
Your story also needs to be eaten one small moment at a time.

Dozen topics VS Egg Topics

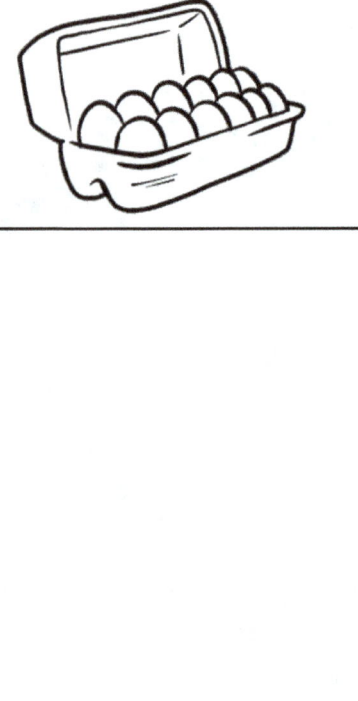

In your journal describe the first image in detail. Write using full sentences in a descriptive paragraph or 2. Do the same for the second image.

WRITING MASTERY

ZOOMING IN

Writers need to zoom in and find those small, beautiful details to add interest to their writing. Similar to the egg and dozen story, writers must find the minute details and add those to the story. Pick a moment that you have planned. Zoom in on the fine details.

⬅ Zooming closer

_____
_____
_____
_____
_____
_____

PROJECT 2

Creative Writing
Find an interesting image in a magazine, 0nline or your private photographs. Describe the whole image in two paragraphs and then in one paragraph, zoom in on one small section of the image and write a description.

WRITING MASTERY

PLANNING

Write the Beginning, Middle, Middle, Middle and End. Use a picture or caption for each section. Use your plan to write your first draft and then type your final draft.

B

M

M

M

E

EXCITING BEGINNINGS

Action

Dialogue

Onomatopoeia

Question

Vivid Description

WRITING MASTERY

PROJECT 3

Scavenger Hunt
Look for exciting beginnings in books, magazine articles or short stories. Create a PowerPoint of slide share of the hooks that you find.

TRANSITION LIST

In the first place
not only ... but also
as a matter of fact
in like manner
in addition
coupled with
in the same fashion / way
first, second, third
in the light of
not to mention
to say nothing of
equally important
too
moreover
as well as
together with
coupled with
furthermore

Categorize the words in the boxes

again
to
and
also
then
equally
identically
uniquely
like
of course
likewise
comparatively
correspondingly
similarly
By the same token

WRITING MASTERY | 26

Transition

Transitions are great for the flow of writing. Write down the transitions you will use for each paragraph of your story. Complete each sentence

Introduction	
First paragraph	
Second Paragraph	
Third Paragraph	
Fourth Paragraph	
Conclusion	

FIRST DRAFT

First Draft Title _____

PROOFREADING TAGS

Use the proofreading tags to edit the paragraph below.
Use them to edit your own writing after you have revised it.

in the, mutopa Kingdom, Princess Onai is getting Ready for her marriage to Prince Gomo when she is cursed by a jealous Trickster and falls into an endless sleep Trapped in the land of dreams!Onai cannot return, unless someone is brave enough to search for her and bring her back. who will this brave warrior be Will he get to her in time!

_____

_____

_____

_____

_____

_____

_____

TYPES OF SENTENCES

As you revise your essay, you need to check the sentences and include a variety of types.

Simple Sentences
A simple sentence consists of one clause and has a subject and a verb. A simple sentence puts across one type of idea.
Declarative: I wrote a story
Imperative: Write your story today.
Interrogative: What are you writing about?
Exclamatory: Your writing is brilliant!

Compound sentence
A type of sentence that contains two independent clauses separated by a conjunction.

FANBOYS
For and nor but or yet so

I wrote my story at school, so I could work on my violin.
I love to write fiction, but I also love to read biographies.

Complex sentence
A type of sentence that contains one independent clause and one dependent clause.

COMMON SUBORDINATING CONJUNCTIONS
AFTER ALTHOUGH BECAUSE IF ONCE UNTIL WHEN WHENEVER

Although I enjoy the creative aspect of writing, I still dread the revision stage.

WRITING MASTERY

MASTERING FIGURATIVE LANGUAGE

The First Day of Spring
The first day of spring
itches
because
an emerald blade of grass
is
pushing out
of
my forehead
I've become
a unicorn

What is this poem about? Write your thoughts in this space.

Pick 4 sentences from your essay and try and re write them using figurative language. Use your tool kit.

1
2
3
4

WRITING MASTERY

PROJECT 4

Figurative Mobile

Crate a mobile of figurative language. You must include at least 8 types of examples. You must also create your own.

THE POWER OF DETAILS

Details using sight, hearing, touch, smell, and taste. Don't forget thinking and feelings.

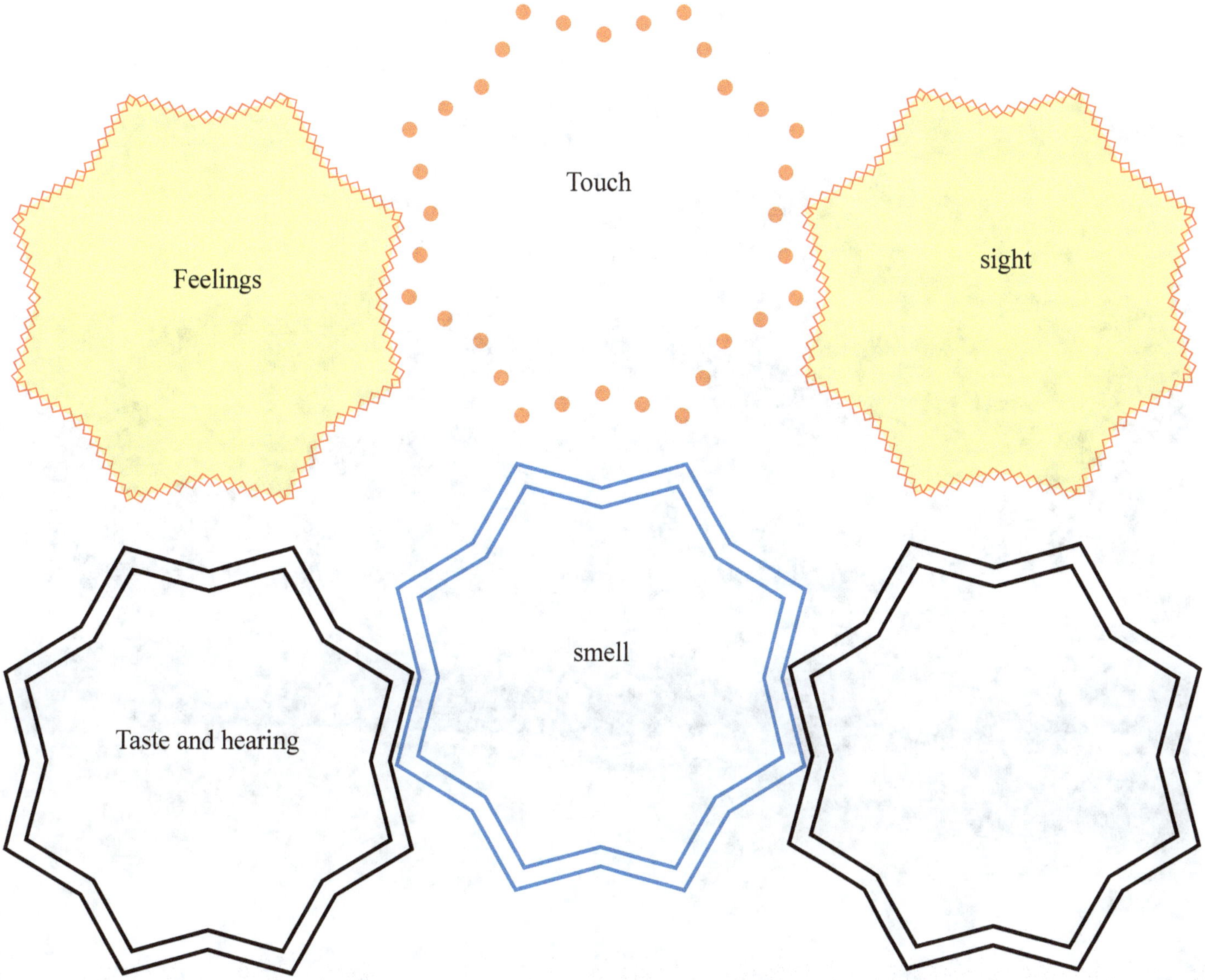

Touch

Feelings

sight

Taste and hearing

smell

WRITING MASTERY | 34

MASTERING SHOW DON'T TELL

Take 3 of your sentences and turn them into showing sentences. Use your writing toolbox. For example

Telling sentence: My room was messy.
Showing Sentence: I climbed over shoes, boxes, and tripped over my keyboard before I reached my bed. I threw all the clothes on the bed to the floor.

SHOW NOT TELL

PROJECT 5

Show Not Tell Book
Create a picture book with hidden flaps. On the top flap you will describe something and underneath, you will draw picture of the thing or event. The idea is that people must guess what you are describing

CONCLUSIONS

How you end your essay is very important. Endings can leave your reader with a great feeling or disappointment. Write down 3 transitional words to use during your ending

_____. _____.

_____.

Write a conclusion for one essay you have done before. Write a conclusion for one essay you have done before.

So What Conclusion

You: Spending time in Disney, especially the moment on the magic carpet ride was a day I will never forget.

Friend: So what?

You: Well, it's I'm important to spend time with family and being on the awesome ride.

Friend: Why should anybody care?

You: Being with family and having such an experience is important because it makes us closer and builds lasting memories that we will look back on when we are also adults and have our own children.

CONCLUSIONS

- *Demonstrate the importance of your ideas*
- *Propel your reader to a new view on the subject*
- *End on a positive note*
- *Leave the reader feeling glad that they read your paper.*

FINAL DRAFT

Using all that you learned write your final draft, your best piece.

Draft Title _____

_____
_____
_____
_____
_____
_____
_____
_____
_____
_____
_____
_____
_____
_____

SAMPLE ESSAY

Use the rubric and checklist to grade this essay. Can it be improved?
Now write your comments. First give the positive comments and then explain what can be improved.

TOPIC

Think about a time when your plans didn't work out. Write a personal narrative about a time when something you wanted failed to work or happen.

"Let's go," Faith, my best friend pulled my arm. I nearly spilled the orange juice on my uniform. I gulped the sticky sweet drink, while holding the tasty jelly sandwich. Stuffing the last bite in my mouth we left the dining hall.

Outside, heat poured over my body as if I had stepped into a sauna while the bread stuck in my throat added to the discomfort. As we ran towards the hall, I tried to clear my throat, but floured lump continued to fill it like an egg was stuck in there. How was I going to sing? It was the day of choir auditions!

With trepidation, I sat on the bench outside the hall listening to the tension of thirty other girls who wanted to make the fifteen-girl choir. Before I could relax, I heard my name, like thunder from the doorway.

"Megan?" Mrs. Millard called in her booming voice. I walked up to the gleaming grand piano and continued to clear my throat. The bread was definitely stuck there and the more I coughed the bigger it grew, like a balloon filling with air. Mrs. Millard strummed the first note to the song. A sound like a croaking frog came out from my mouth. My eyes bulged out and the urge to scream shook me. Trembling, I touched the burning skin by my throat and felt my eyes water. Mrs. Millard stared at me as she had just seen a cat driving a car. Her eyes doubled in size and she shook her head as if to get rid of a spider stuck in her white curly hair.

"Want to try again?" she asked and started the note again leaning on the piano like a giraffe about to drink water. My mouth opened and this time I clearly sounded like an ant that had swallowed a frog. I continued to sing and I could see the pain on Mrs. Millard's face as she played the piano and listened to the worst voice in the history of choir auditions. She stopped in the middle of the verse and tried to smile at me, but I could see a wince instead. "Thank you, Megan. I will post the results tomorrow."

As I walked away I knew that my days in the choir were over and tears stung my eyes. This was so many years ago, but I still remember the pain like it was yesterday. I regretted eating the sandwich and wished I had drunk some water soon after to clear my throat passage. Being in the choir made me happy and I thought I had a good voice. Unfortunately, since then, I don't consider myself a singer anymore.

RESOURCES

Exciting Beginnings

dialolgue
"When the lion comes close, you must not stare at him," my mom said.

action
The lion leapt from the tree and landed next to the car.

Question
If you could be an animal, which one would you choose?

onomatopoeia
Stomp! Stomp! the elephants marched past the tree.

Examples of hooks

description
As the golden sunlight closed its eyes, the grass turned brown and the lions began to move.

quote
With each new day in Africa, a gazelle wakes up knowing he must outrun the fastest lion or perish.

CONGRATULATIONS!

You have finished the first course. You will receive a certificate of completion if you get 80% or higher on your final essay.

FINAL ESSAY TEST

Please complete the essay below and submit by email or google docs.

Personal Narrative Final Exam

> "I've learned one thing in life, it's: Stand for something or you will fall for anything."
> Bonnie Hunt.

Essay Topic

Think about a time you stood for what you believed in. Be sure to share with your reader what the situation was like, what happened when you stood your ground, and what happened as a result.

Be sure to
- describe the events of the experience with a clear focus
- provide a clear, beginning, middle and end.
- Describe how this experience affected you.

www.ingramcontent.com/pod-product-compliance
Lightning Source LLC
Chambersburg PA
CBHW080834010526
44112CB00016B/2514